A Journey of Faith

Life Through My Eyes

Anthony Fahey

A Journey of Faith
Life Through My Eyes

All rights reserved. This book or any portion thereof may not be reproduced or used in any manner whatsoever without the express written permission of the authors except for the use of brief quotations in a book review or scholarly journal.

Book Completion Services Provided by:
TRU Statement Publications
www.trustatementpublications.com

Copyright © 2020 Anthony Fahey
First Printing: 2020,
Printed in the United States of America
06192020
ISBN-13: 978-1-948085-39-7

DEDICATION

This book is dedicated to all who carry the Fahey name in hopes that the name lives on for generations to come.

ACKNOWLEDGEMENT

First and foremost, I must acknowledge the Lord Jesus Christ for giving me the wisdom to write and complete this book. If it were not for His grace, I would not have been able to do so. I thank him for blessing me with the knowledge, the understanding, the clarity of thought, and the wisdom to put all of this together. All of the thanks, praise, and glory goes to my Lord Jesus Christ.

I thank my wife Brenda for her support and understanding, as I woke up early each day to continue writing and for just being there for me as I wrote this book.

I thank my daughter Desiree for her input, her assistance, her guidance, and her organizational skills, as it was instrumental to me for the completion of this book.

I thank Apostle Jarvis Hines and First Lady Vanessa of Consuming Fire Ministries International for their spiritual guidance in the preparation of this book, reminding me that the completion of this book was made possible through the grace of our Lord Jesus Christ.

I thank Evangelist Karen Gates of Consuming Fire Ministries International for introducing me to the right people who was able to take this book from the draft form and put it into print. May the good Lord bless her for her kindness and assistance.

I thank my family members Freddie Julien, Evril Fahey, Earl Fahey, Felix Fahey, Ann Fahey-Questal, and Yvette Fahey-Bebe, for the background information that I received from them.

I would like to thank my friend Ramkissoon (Chone) Ramroop for the info that he gave me about the time we were learning our trades together and for giving me the moral support during that period of time.

I would like to thank Cousin Jean Tippett (Cupcake) for her assistance in helping me to organize my pictures in the book.

Lastly, I would like to honorably mention the following family members who over the years had given information that I have used in the writing of this book. Unfortunately, they are deceased and are no longer with us, but the information that I received from them was vital. They are grandpa Charles Coombs, my mother Hermina Fahey, my dad Trevor Fahey, and my uncle Preston Coombs.

"Now faith is the substance of the things hoped for, the evidence of things not seen."

Hebrews 11:1

CONTENTS

DEDICATION i
CONTENTS ix
FOREWORD xii
INTRODUCTION xiii
MY GRANDFATHER 1
EARLY RESEARCH 7
DAD TALKING ABOUT MOM 11
FREDDIE'S RECOLLECTION OF MOM 15
MY UNCLE PRESTON 19
MY SIBLINGS STORIES 25
LIFE ON THE ESTATE 29
LEAVING THE ESTATE 33
LIFE AFTER LEAVING THE ESTATE 39
FINALLY, WATER AND POWER 43
MAKING ENDS MEET 45
SCHOOL/COLLEGE 47
MY FIRST JOB 49
BAD ADVICE 53
OFFICER OF THE LAW 59
FAMILY LIFE 65
MY HERO 69
ACCIDENTS 71
FORESIGHT 75

HONESTY	77
LOYALTY	79
FORGIVENESS	81
DISCOVERY	85
MIGRATION TO THE U.S.	91
FIRST U.S. JOB	97
MILITARY TIME	101
DEATH OF MY FATHER	107
DEATH OF MY MOTHER	113
THE WAKE	119
THE BIG "C"	121
EFFECTS OF 9/11	127
CATHOLICISM	135
CHRISTIAN FAITH	139
DEATH OF MY GRANDSON	141
MEMORIES	145
BAPTISM	149
BIBLIOGRAPHY	153

FOREWORD

I am honored to be a part of a book written by my brother, and friend, Anthony (Tony) Fahey and to compose a Foreword for this book. This book is a must read as it deals with a man that I consider to be a Servant, Soldier, Survivor, and a Saint who left his country of Trinidad, in the West Indies, with nothing to came to the United States.

Tony became a soldier in our military and served our country. He was a working man, a Heavy-Duty Mechanic/Welder in the mines of Nevada. He contracted cancer and survived it. He is a saint and a strong believer in God. To see a man who came from another country, and knew no one, to becoming a high-ranking soldier, cancer survivor, and stayed strong in his faith is an achievement in itself.

I highly recommend that you read this book, as it will let you know, it is not where you start, but where you finish and how you survive the journey.

INTRODUCTION

I have a unique family history and wanted to share my history with the current, younger, generation of the Fahey family. I believe that everyone should strive to know where they came from, for it is important to know who we are as a family and how we began. This book will provide them with that information insuring that this knowledge will not be lost.

MY GRANDFATHER

My grandfather, Charles Coombs, was a tall thin man with salt and pepper hair. He lost some hair from the top front of his head, but it did not take away from the fact that he was a handsome man for his age. For many years, I asked my grandfather for information about my mom and grandmother. I was yet to understand why he did not want to speak to me before about my mom. Over the years I had only heard little bits and pieces from different family members as to where mom had come from, her family, and what happened to my grandmother, my mom's mother.

Finally, one day, when my grandfather was about 60 years old, I managed to pin him down. What transpired then was very enlightening, and I believe it to be an amazing story of my mom and my grandmother.

My grandfather sat me down and said that he originally

came from Barbados, in the Caribbean. Work on that island, in those days, was not too lucrative; so, after learning there was going to be a lot of work on the mainland of Venezuela, building roads that led into the interior of the country, he decided to go and seek employment over there.

At the time he was single, so leaving Barbados was not a problem. He said he did get employment in Venezuela, working on the roads outside of Caracas. He worked with many other workers who came from other parts of Venezuela and from other islands within the Caribbean. Camps were set up close to the roads they were building, so that the workers would have a place to stay when they were not at work.

As the roads progressed, the camps got too far away from the work site. The camps were broken down and moved closer to the work site. This process would repeat itself as the work continued. Grandpa said the work was hard, tiring, dirty, and long. The work took them close to the river and the jungle, which caused them to be besieged with irritating bugs.

People from villages who were close by, and even far away, came to the camp to offer their services for hire. The workers could get the villagers to do their washing, cooking, and cleaning of their living areas, so that when they came home, after a long day of work, their clothes were washed and they had a hot meal waiting for them.

Grandpa said he hired this one group of people to take care of him. Because they were all from the same family, he had to take them all; one can only hire them if you were willing to hire the whole family. So, he hired the father, mother, and daughter. He said this group were from the *Buck Tribe*. They were called this because they were Spanish speaking Venezuelan Indians, who wandered about the countryside selling their wares and services.

The workers called them gypsies or aborigines who lived in the area, but they never stayed too long in any one area and called no village their home. This arrangement worked out fine for my grandfather, because at the end of the workday he would be very tired and did not feel like washing, cooking, and cleaning his area, all he wanted was a meal, a shower and a place to lie down and sleep.

Sometime during their employment with him, he got involved with the daughter of the leader of the tribe or family. She became pregnant, which was fine with him and the family, or so he believed. During the pregnancy, the family stayed at the camp with him and continued to do all the chores at his place in the camp.

About six months after the baby, my mother, was born, he returned to camp one day after work and found the baby asleep, wrapped in a blanket, and lying in his bed. The family was gone, leaving without explanation. They simply disappeared. My grandfather said he tried to find her family, he made inquiries in and around the campsite and at nearby villages. But these searches came up with nothing. They were never found, seen, or heard of again; they simply just disappeared into the jungle, or maybe they took the river and moved on to another part of the Delta.

At the time, my grandfather had no one to care for the baby while he was at work, so he decided to leave that job and return to Trinidad, where my mom was later brought up. When asked how he felt back then about the family, he said he had no ill feelings towards my grandmother or her family, only sadness over the fact that she had left without saying goodbye to him. When asked how he felt now, after all those years had gone by, he said, "I really loved your grandmother and her family. I often wondered where she was and what became of her and her family. I know in my heart she is thinking of your mother and me, and that she loves us both."

Then with a look of what I believe to be sadness in his face, and in a low tone of voice he said, "Son that is the story of your mother, remember it!" With that said, our little talk was over; he said there was nothing else he had to add to the story or to say on the matter.

Maybe the talk with my grandfather left him with a sense of closure as to my mom's roots, and with a bit of sadness at the fact that mom never got to know her mother. My mom grew up and accepted the fact that she would never get to meet her mom or get to ever know her, but I know that sometimes she thinks of her mom, because there are times when she was observed being very quiet and seemed to be lost in thought. During those times, we believed that she was thinking of her mom and wishes that she were around to see her grow up to become a wonderful woman, wife, and mother with children of her own.

EARLY RESEARCH

I have always wanted to find out more about mom's roots, and over the years I have spoken to her, on several occasions, trying to find out what she could tell me about her mother. She said she could not tell me anything, because she was too young then and could not remember anything about her mom or her family. All she could remember is what she was told, that she is from the Buck Tribe.

As I continued my research, trying to find out more about her family and the Buck Tribe, all my research and inquiries were unsuccessful. During that time, I believed the Buck Tribe was the last of their kind, because they did not call any village their home and they were not registered anywhere or with any village. I could not find any record of their existence.

During my investigation, I encountered a high-ranking government official from Venezuela. He informed me that when he was in college, he did his thesis on Venezuelan Gypsies/Aborigines. He said that he had heard of the Buck Tribe and had made inquiries about them, but he could not find any record of their existence. He did say that he believed they really did exist, however all his inquires to locate them proved fruitless, for he could not find any information about their whereabouts.

He believed as I did, they had simply just disappeared somewhere into the interior of Venezuela never to be heard of again. Between the both of us, though we believed this was only speculation for not having anything more concrete to go on, we would not be able to completely or accurately confirm what really happened to my mom's family and the Buck Tribe.

I asked him if he had an explanation as to why they left the baby and just went away. He said that during his research, the information he received while observing and speaking to members of other tribes in the area, was the baby was not a full blooded member of the tribe, as a result they just left her and went away. He said this may not be common practice with us, normal or civilized people, but we have to remember that those people lived a far different way of life from us, and to them, this was probably normal behavior and a part of their lifestyle.

At that time, we believed we may have never found out anything more about her heritage, so that part of mom's family was pretty much closed to us. We then believed that my mom and her family would remain my family's secret or mystery.

EARLY RESEARCH

DAD TALKING ABOUT MOM

I remember asking dad to tell me what he knew about mom and her family. He said that he had accepted the fact that she came from Venezuela and that he loved her dearly. He did not want to pursue her heritage.

To him it did not matter where she came from and he had accepted her just the way she was. I did not get any more information from him about her.

In my time today, I would definitely want to know more about my wife's family, but I guess in my dad's time he did not deem it important enough to want to find out more about her heritage.

Maybe, somehow, he knew it was futile for him to do so; anyway he was satisfied with how things were and did not want to find out anything more about her that would change how he felt about her, for he had accepted her just the way she was and finding out her heritage did not matter to him. No further information was forthcoming from him, so that was all I could get from him.

FREDDIE'S RECOLLECTION OF MOM

I remember talking with my elder brother, Freddie Julien, about what he remembered about mom's heritage. He was my brother by my mom only and did not have the same dad as I. He was of medium build, thin, not too muscular, or tall, had a fair complexion, and graying hair.

He knew much more than I did about mom, but it took a very long time for us to get together and talk about her and where she came from. Freddie said all that he knows about mom was what my grandfather, Charles Coombs, told him. He said grandpa told him that while he was in Venezuela working on building roads, he remembered seeing people living on the banks of the river in houses with thatched roof, which only had a floor, no sides, and the houses were built, on what he called, stilts or poles.

Later, at the camp where the workers were staying, some of the people from other areas, would come to the camp to sell their wares and to seek work. He said he hired a family to cook, clean, and wash his clothes. He said he eventually got involved with the daughter of the family that was working for him, got her pregnant, and mom was born while he was there.

Sometime later the family left the area leaving the baby on his bed in the camp and went away. He was never able to find them. After that, my grandfather said he believed that my mom's family was of the Buck Tribe because these people lived in that area.

It seemed that every time I spoke to a member of my family about mom's heritage, a different story of her early life emerged. It has left me even more puzzled.

Freddie said that was all he could remember about mom, and what he knew was what he was told about her. This was just a little more information that I received, as I continued my investigation into my parent's heritage.

When asked about my dad, as far as my brother could remember, Freddie said he knew that dad was born in Trinidad. His parents came from Ireland and they grew up in Trinidad. He did not have any more information on that part of the family, mainly because they were not close to us.

That side of the family was closed off to us, they did not want anything to do with us and this was mainly because dad, being Caucasian, had married mom who they considered black. He remembered the animosity that existed between dad and his family, but he had no more info to add to that side of the family's heritage.

When asked if he could explain to me why they were so prejudicial towards us, he put it this way, "Some people of Caucasian descent, like dad's family, believe they are the true race and black people, like us, are nothing. That is what they believe, and as a result, they do not want to be around us and there is nothing we can do to make them change the way they feel."

I should mention that, after dad passed, Freddie was the one who mostly drove dad's car, but that did not last too long because one day he got in an accident and totally wrecked the car.

Needless to say, that was the end of the car. I think if dad was still around, he would have some choice words for Freddie for destroying his *baby,* as he called his car.

MY UNCLE PRESTON

Sometime around February 2016, I had the opportunity to speak to my uncle Preston about my mom. I wanted to find out what he knew about mom and her life. It was sad that after all these years I was finally able to talk to him. It was unfortunate in the sense that he was now terminal, having suffered a long time with cancer of the lung and kidneys. The cancer had run its course and there was nothing else the doctors could do for him.

He was my uncle, for he and mom had the same dad. It was a very difficult visit for me. He was always a strong person, hardworking, and very family oriented. He was tall and muscular. He had short graying black hair and he had a small punch around the middle. I used to kid him about his food intake, because he was a healthy eater and could easily put away a large meal, but he was not fat; he had more muscles than fat.

To see him weak, unable to walk even a short distance from the living room to the restroom, which was only one room away, was a challenge for him. He could not do anything without the aid of oxygen. He wore a nasal cannula and had to walk around with an oxygen tank on wheels, which was hard for him, but he managed to maneuver it without too much difficulty.

He was sitting on a couch in the living room when I came into his house. He teared up when he saw me and stood up, although it took much effort for him to do so. We hugged for a long time. I could feel his body shake. As we stood there, he tried to hold back the tears, but we both just let it flow. As we chatted, I saw him not as the uncle who was terminal, but as the strong family man I knew him to be. He was still there for his family and he had accepted the fact that he was not going to be around too much longer.

Uncle Preston was cool, quiet, yet reserved. He had an inner peace with himself that I saw in his eyes, and I knew he was ready for whatever came next. He had taken care of, and made all the arrangements for his homecoming, or departure, from this life. He somehow seemed to know that he was going on to a better life. For me, that took a great degree of strength and faith.

We talked about a lot of things that day. Not too much about his illness, because we both knew the end result of that, and he wanted to keep a positive mental attitude in front of his wife. So, we talked about his job at the hospital, his love for steel band music, and the pan side that he owned. Those were fun days he remembered, and it brought a smile to his face. He owned a steel band side so called because it is a group of musicians who played music on steel drums together; they were called a steel band side.

He loved to play mas during carnival time and did that for many years too. During carnival, he took his band to the streets and played mas. It is called "playing mas" because revelers would dress up in costumes and parade and dance to the sound of steel band music as they played the latest music at that time.

I believed Uncle Preston had a good life, for he was smiling quite a bit. He said he had to be strong for his wife and had to show her that he appreciated her and everything she had done for him. He was always thinking of his family. What I saw that day in him was the legacy of love for his family. He was going to leave behind a legacy that I can emulate in my own life in remembrance of him.

I eventually brought up the subject of my mom's heritage and asked him what he remembered about her, his half-sister by father only. It is sad, because he knew that I wanted information about my mom, but for years he did not want to talk to me about her. I did not understand what the big secret was. I think, now that he was terminal, he probably wanted to clear his conscience.

Uncle Preston said his dad had told him years ago that mom was born in Venezuela and that she belonged to the Warao people who lived in the area close to where he was working. He also said my grandfather told him that he fathered another child who was born in Venezuela, his name was Phillipe. Years later he tried finding Phillipe but was unable to locate him. So, I guess I have another uncle that may still be living somewhere out there in Venezuela.

Uncle Preston said that was all that he could remember of what his dad had told him, and he did not have anything else to add about mom's heritage. He was just repeating what his dad had told him.

MY UNCLE PRESTON

Three weeks after speaking with him about this, he passed. I believe he went to be with the Lord. May the good Lord take him into His fold.

MY SIBLINGS STORIES

I continued my research and spoke to all my siblings, Evril, Earl, Felix, Ann, and Yvette, because I wanted to find out what they could remember about mom and dad's early life. They all told me what they could remember.

The stories I got from them was what they had learned after they grew up. They were young then, so what they know was passed down from other family members, to them.

What they all believed is that mom was born in Venezuela and came to live in Trinidad. Mom's dad was from Barbados, an island in the Caribbean.

MY SIBLINGS STORIES

About dad, he was born in Trinidad and grew up there. His parents were immigrants from Ireland and they also lived in Trinidad.

My siblings did not know how our parents met. They only became aware of them being married when they were much older, so that part of our parent's early life was not known to us. They know that they were their parents for they all turned out well and had a good life, thanks to their wonderful parents.

MY SIBLINGS STORIES

LIFE ON THE ESTATE

This is my recollection of my early childhood growing up and living on the estate. We lived on an estate plantation consisting about 250 acres of land which cultivated the main crops of cocoa and coffee with secondary crops of bananas, plantains, mangoes, coconut, and oranges. We also had a herd of goats numbering about 100, which was used for food and for selling to the public for additional income.

I remember how the cocoa and coffee beans were transported when the cocoa pods and the coffee beans were ripe and ready to be harvested. The workers would gather them up and bring them to a determined collection point in the field. The cocoa pods were opened, and the beans were taken out of the pod. The coffee beans were picked and was also taken to the collection point. They were then loaded into two large baskets, one for the cocoa seeds and the other for the coffee beans. These baskets were strapped onto the back of our donkey, who in turn transported it from the collection point in the field to the drying house at the big house.

The drying house was a building with a flat deck. All the beans were spread out on the floor. The roof was made onto rails, so that on sunny days the roof was rolled back to let the sun in and on rainy days the roof was rolled back to cover the beans, so they would not get wet.

I found it amazing that the donkey was trained to make the

trip back and forth on its own, without any guidance, of a distance about one eighth of a mile. One of the workers had to walk with the donkey, only once in the morning, and then the donkey made the rest of the trips for that day on its own.

We also raised chickens and we used the eggs for food. We lived in a 4-bedroom house that was comfortable and roomy. We had a 12-Volt DC generator that ran on kerosene fuel which provided power to the house. Dad only ran the generator from dust to bedtime, then he turned it off and kerosene lamps with attached reflectors were used for light for the rest of the night. We also had indoor running water and an indoor bathroom.

I don't think we were rich, but we were considered very well off, and while living there we had everything we wanted and lacked nothing. We even had servants who worked in the house, cooked, and cleaned for us.

I remember dad had a Morris Minor Station Wagon. It was British, made sometime in the 1960s. How he acquired it, I do not know, but it was very nice. He also owned a Thames Trader truck that he used to transport different types of materials from the quarry and the crusher to his clients. We had a lot of people working for us, in and out of the house, in the cocoa and coffee plantation, taking care of the herd of goats, working in the yellow stone quarry, and operating the crusher with all of the equipment, like a yellow Ford Farmal and a bulldozer that they used to keep this operation going. There was also a blue stone quarry, but that type of rock was not too popular back then.

I believe we had a good childhood, with really nothing to do, for everything was done for us. We had no chores to do, we just had to go to school at that time. It was a good life for us, very laid back and things continued that way for many years.

LEAVING THE ESTATE

In the early 1960s the estate plantation was sold. It brought us back down to reality when we had to pack up our personal belongings and move out of the estate house and plantation. It was hard on us, for we never thought we would ever have to leave the estate and go somewhere else to live. Until then, it was the only life we knew, and we never thought we would have to move and give up this way of life.

LEAVING THE ESTATE

We moved to a small village about 15 miles away and dad had to build us a house to live in. He also had to seek employment wherever he could find it so he could keep food on the table. Dad worked driving trucks. He worked operating a dredge, clearing a waterway so boats could come closer to the shore to pick up supplies in Trinidad. He also did the same work in St Vincent, another nearby island in the Caribbean. He went and worked wherever he could find a job.

Looking back now, I believe that my father should have had a little more foresight. He never thought about the future, he just thought about the moment. I remember the many parties that were held at the house and all the drinking and eating that took place. Yes, my folks sure had a good time then, but in life, it is necessary and good practice that we always put something away for a rainy day.

Dad did not do that, maybe because he thought he would do it later or that he also thought that this lifestyle would go on for many more years to come, and that he would do it then. I do not know; all I know is that he never did it. When we had to leave the estate, dad did not have much savings, so in our new place, life was not easy at all.

We had to accept the fact that we no longer had the things we had back then and could no longer live like we did on the estate. It was not a good time for us, but dad made us stick together as a family and we survived; but for me, it was like starting over. For all I knew before then was the easy life.

The house that dad built is still standing today. It has 4 bedrooms, and at that time we had no power. Our lights were kerosene lamps with attached reflectors. There was no running water in the house. We had to get water from a spring and bring it to the house to be used for drinking and cooking. I learned to balance a bucket of water on my head as I made the trip from the spring to the house several times a day, like before and after school and on weekends. It was probably a distance of about a quarter of a mile, but I got used to it.

For washing, mom used rainwater that ran off the roof and collected in drums and a cistern. The latrine or outhouse, for doing our business, was terrible. It was out back a little way from the house. In the daytime, it was not too bad because you could see what you were doing, but if you had to use it in the nighttime, it was totally different. It was dark and we had to use a light that we made from a bottle filled with kerosene. We put a cloth wick in it, flipped it over, and when it was soaked with kerosene, we lit it, and that provided enough light for us to do our business.

When the outhouse was full, a man came and dug a hole next to the latrine and moved the little house over the new hole so that we would have a new and empty place in which to do our business; the outhouse was all one piece. The old hole was covered up and left there. After a long time, the feces dried up. So, I guess that was normal back then and it was how they got rid of the feces.

Now, if you were afraid of bullfrogs you should not be, for they are harmless, just scary looking. There was a lot of them and some folks did not like them, so they had to carry a stick in their hand to push them out of the way so they could pass on their way to the outhouse. They had to do it again when they left. It seemed as though they loved to just sit on the path to the latrine.

I was not afraid of them, but I did the same thing to them with the stick. Now why they liked just sitting there on the path, I do not know, but you could always find them there every night. It was as though they were waiting for something, but I never understood what they were waiting for or why they did it, and what caused them to display this odd behavior. So, we accepted them as being a part of the country life and left them alone. We lived like this in the house for several years.

LIFE AFTER LEAVING THE ESTATE

I missed many years of mom's early life and have no information about how my mom and dad met. I can only jump ahead to the time when I was growing up. We lived and grew up in the home with both of them.

As far as my dad is concerned, my inquiries revealed that he was born in Woodbrook, a suburb in the capital, Port of Spain, Trinidad. From parents who migrated from Ireland, they were of course, Caucasian. I grew up to believe that my dad was born in Ireland, but he was actually born in Trinidad, so he had some Irish blood in his veins.

When I was younger, I remember my dad's mom and dad. There were issues when mom and dad got married, because dad did not marry a Caucasian woman as they wanted him to do. Over the years, his decision to marry my mom, a Venezuelan

Aborigine Indian, who his family considered to be black had plagued him, but he decided to stick with her no matter what.

My grandfather died of a heart attack and my grandmother eventually remarried to a gentleman who did not care too much for us, mainly because of my mom. I believe he had personal racial issues. In reality, mom was short with a brown, light skinned complexion which was taken from her tribe. My dad's family, including my grandmother's new husband, did not want my grandmother associating with us. He prevented her from having any connection with us. I think mainly because two of our brothers came out light skinned, just like mom, and the other two brothers and two sisters took after dad and came out Caucasian looking, just like him; but through it all, my dad stuck with mom and us.

No matter what the family said, it did not matter to him, long ago he had made his decision to be with our mom, and there was nothing anyone could do to change that. Dad stood up for us and all I have to say is, "Go dad, you're the man!"

Afterwards, dad told us that there are all kinds of different people in this world with different points of views, and there is nothing we can really do about it; except, to try to not be like those folks who harbor ill feelings towards people who maybe of a different race or color. He said we need to forgive them, because most of the time they are just ignorant and says things that can be hurtful to others, for whatever comes out of their mouths also comes out from their hearts; that is how they feel and that is what is hard to change.

When I found out the reason why they did not want to be around us, it bothered me for a number of years; but like dad, I found it in my heart to forgive them too. It was depressing to me to be that way because I believe in family sticking together and living together as one. I should mention that it is sad to say, after all those years, they did not change their opinion of us and have never accepted us into that side of the family, but that is okay, for we have lived with it and have forgiven them all.

FINALLY, WATER AND POWER

Finally, dad was financially able to have commercial power put into the house and had running water also hooked up to the house. I must say that was a good day, for we no longer had to carry water from the spring to the house. We all thanked him for doing that. Water in the pipeline was left up to the water company to provide to us. It was not too often, so we had to get those large storage water tanks so we could have water for the house when none was provided by the water company.

Water would come through the pipes, maybe two or three times a week, to fill up the tanks. When the water did come, everyone in the village had to do the same thing too. After all these years, the practice of waiting on water to come through the pipelines has not changed. If you take a drive through the villages, you will see that everyone has at least two water tanks in their homes to collect water when it comes through the pipe lines.

MAKING ENDS MEET

Dad bought himself a used car that he used for transportation for work. I must give him credit though, for he worked hard to provide for us, keep us clothed and to put food on the table. He was quite an outstanding man and a remarkable and loving dad. Although we were living differently, and things were tough, I never saw my dad complain or give up. He just kept on moving ahead. He said we were his number one priority. He made us aware of this, and he had no regrets about doing what he did for us.

Mom ensured that we profess our love to dad and showed him our appreciation for all that he did for us. I am sure that in doing so, it helped to give him that extra drive to do so much more, knowing that his family was behind him in everything he did.

Living in this new village, we had a comfortable life and accepted things as they were. To help out, we raised pigs, which we slaughtered on weekends and sold to villagers for additional income. We also raised chickens which we used for food and planted a garden which provided us with fruits like, coconuts, vegetables, and ground provisions like, dasheen cassava, eddoes, and tania. Some of the things that came from the garden were mangoes, avocados, ochoa, pumpkin, breadfruit, limes, lemons, guava, plums, and oranges. We had lots to eat and to be thankful for, and with the occasional fresh fish we bought, our meals were very well balanced.

SCHOOL/COLLEGE

I attended a nearby Hindu school and graduated from it. Many years later, I visited the area and surprisingly that school is still standing in the same place, and it looks just the same way now and how I remember it back then, in the early 1960s. With the neatly painted siding and walls, the well-kept drains and walkways, and the beautiful well-manicured rows of flowerbeds on the sides and back of the building, brought me memories of those early school days that laid dormant in my mind.

It took a visit to see the school again, although I was not allowed to enter because it was fenced in and there was a security guard on the premises to prevent vandalism to the property, to bring back those memories to me, and for me to remember those happy carefree days.

SCHOOL/COLLEGE

As I developed my learning, knowledge, and abilities I attended a college and obtained a two-year degree, but dad could not afford to continue paying for me to finish my education, and I had to drop out and go to work helping him on his truck. So that he did not have to pay another loader, I took his place and the money that he would have had to pay him. Dad kept that money and it came back into the home to help pay bills and buy food for us. Yes, I was disappointed, for I wanted to stay in college, but dad said that was impossible to make happen, so I just accepted what he said, and that was the end of my college education.

Many years later, I was able to complete my college education, but that was when I left the country and lived abroad in the U.S.

MY FIRST JOB

My very first job was working on the road filling and patching potholes, which there were many; but this job was short lived. When I got paid, that money was just enough for me to purchase an outfit. It made me feel good to know that I worked, got paid, and was able to buy myself clothes. My paycheck was $120.00 every two weeks. To me, that was a lot of money for someone who never got a paycheck before.

Sometime in the late 1960s, I began to learn a trade with a friend of mine, Ramkissoon (Chone) Ramroop, who lived close to me. We both decided to work and learn these trades together, which were welding, auto body repair, painting, and mechanical auto repair. At first when we started, the money we received was only $1.00 at the end of the week, which was ridiculous, but we learned how to weld and to fabricate things like metal gates and burglar proofing for windows.

As we got better at our jobs, we moved on to another one. This time doing auto body repair, which was more lucrative because we would take a job to complete the body work on a vehicle and when we were done, we would get paid the agreed upon price that was set for that particular job. Eventually, our income moved up to several hundred dollars a week. When we got good at the jobs we were doing, and we were able to work together on our own, and not for someone else, we became knowledgeable and experienced mechanic auto body repairmen and welders.

My friend, Chone, moved on to other things and so did I, but over the years we kept in contact with each other and still maintained that close relationship today. For a while, he continued in his field and I stayed in mine. Today, living in the U.S., my experience has helped me obtain employment in those fields. I continued to work in them until I retired.

Looking back now, I think we made an excellent choice when we decided to get into these trades. I have learned that not all of us can work in the professional fields and that those of us who cannot make it there will work in the skilled crafts fields that are available. It takes all of us working together in our different fields, on any project, to make it happen.

MY FIRST JOB

BAD ADVICE

When I was younger and living at home with my parents, I believed that my mom gave me some bad advice when she refused to let me take music lessons. She gave me many reasons why she would not allow me to learn music. The reasons varied and covered just about everything she could think of.

She would say things like, "You will spend too much time away from home and family. You will return home too late from music school to do your chores around the house. You need to find a job to help pay the bills at home, for music will not do that for you. You cannot support a family by playing music. Instead, you should be doing something more constructive with your time. It is more important to buy clothes and shoes for you than it is to purchase a musical instrument and I could not afford to pay for your transportation from home, to the music center, and back. There are too many young men hanging around the center just waiting to get you into trouble."

Mom was set in, what I believe to be, her old fashioned ways, but I still tried to tell her that learning music was good for me, it teaches discipline and the appreciation of the arts. I can learn a new skill and also learn how to interact with other musicians, also I could have a chance to record and sell my own music if I wanted to, and can have a good and decent life doing that. My mother would not listen to any of my reasons for me wanting to play music.

Many times, I went down to the Music Center without telling her, but that only resulted in a good beating when I got back home. She found out after a few of those sessions, which ended in other beatings. I stopped going there and finally resigned myself to be what she called a good kid. I listened to her and gave up my plans to be a musician, but still I had the choice to continue learning music as I got older, but never took it, for at that time in my life I was involved in other things like living and raising a family.

My mom grew up in a home with her dad and, I believe, her stepmom. They seldom played music in her home; she did not even have a radio until much later in life. Her father did not believe in playing music in the house, not even a radio. He reasoned that instead of listening to the radio you could be doing something more important like chores around the house and working in the garden. She, like her parents before her, reasoned that if she could grow up without music in her life, then I should be able to do the same. She must have gotten that idea from her dad.

Mom did give me a lot of reasons why music was not a good way to earn a living and I eventually went in a different direction in life; but, as I look back I can now see that my mom did give me some bad advice when she did not permit me to study music. Now that part of the music industry that I wanted to get into has grown tremendously into a big industry, and everyone who is associated with it, is making enough money to enjoy a good life.

At that time, my uncle had a steel band side and was willing to teach me music and how to play a tune on a steel pan, but that, too, I was not able to do. She would not ever let me study music with my own uncle, who wanted to teach me. I could have been a part of it, but on the other hand, being young and living at home I did not have any other choice but to listen to my mom, trust her judgment and hope that she had made one that was in my best interest.

Looking back now, I can say that mom did give me some bad advice when she told me that music will not get me anywhere in life. With the utmost respect to my mom, although she did not allow me to study music, I must say that I have learned that children who are not given the opportunity to expand their minds, through music and other fields of interest because of their parents belief and superstition, can have an adverse effect on their lives. I believe parents should make every effort to encourage, promote, and support their children in whatever field of study they are interested in. Do not suppress a child's eagerness to explore new things. A good legacy to pass on to your children is that they should always strive to learn new things, and as a result, they will live a more fulfilling and rewarding life. All was not lost; my heart and my mind are at peace, because I forgave her.

As an adult, I had the choice to get into the music industry, but I did not take up playing any musical instrument, although I own a guitar and a steel pan that my uncle gave me. I never learned to play either one of those instruments. I could have learned to play them, but the drive left me long ago, and now these instruments are just sitting at home collecting dust. They are memories of a time gone by, and I considered them as collectables.

BAD ADVICE

OFFICER OF THE LAW

One of my first good jobs was the one where I became a Police Officer. Several weeks after entering the academy, my training was cut short, because during that time the country was experiencing political unrest and turmoil. This unrest prompted the people to openly express demonstrations resulting in a lot of property damage and personal injuries.

We, the new recruits, had to go out on patrol to protect life and property. On occasions, we would come upon the demonstrators, and if they were too disorderly or were causing any type of property damage or injury to anyone, then we had to take action and disperse the crowd. One efficient method was for us to enter into the crowd in force and remove individuals who were deemed to be the leaders, and as a result of the leaders being taken into custody, the crowd would disperse. It got to a point where we would only have to show up and the crowd would disperse.

There were times when we came upon people we knew or even siblings in the crowd. That made it difficult for those of us who were placed in that position, but we figured out that it was best to ignore them, or have another trainee confront them. We had a job to do, and no matter who they were, we had to do what was right in the eyes of the law. Eventually, this unrest ended.

I graduated from training and moved on to my first duty station, which was the start of a new chapter in my life. I was looking forward to really making a name for myself by being the best investigator I could be. My first assignment was at a small station in a relatively small town. I thought to myself that it would be great. It would be laid-back duty, which means that I would be able to get right into learning how to run a station and how to deal with the public and handling their concerns.

This duty did not turn out as expected; as a matter of fact, nothing prepared me for what I was about to experience. Normally, the station was manned with several officers and we would have to deal with whatever complaint that presented itself through the doors. Each day was different, and one could not imagine what new problem would come through the doors of the station house on any given day.

What made a lasting impression on me, and is worth mentioning here, was the number of cases I investigated that dealt with the loss of life. I think I saw the many faces of death. It is hard to believe that in a small town like this, there would be so much violence and death. During my first few years, I came upon death from traffic accidents, suicides, and saw victims of murders from gunshots, hanging, stabbings, and choppings.

I recall witnessing my first of many autopsies. It was a murder/suicide. This person had stabbed the first victim many, many, times; he shot the second victim several times with a shotgun at point blank range, and then committed suicide with a shotgun blast to his head. This autopsy was very upsetting. I could not comprehend how a young person could commit such a violent and senseless murderous act.

I remember afterwards that day, not having an appetite for food and having a hard time falling asleep that night. Those were violent incidents that caused me to do a lot of soul searching. Life is short, and I remember thinking that there's got to be more to life than all this violence. This was a very depressing time for me, but I had to remember and accept the fact that this was not a very big country, and in many ways, violence was a way of life over here.

I still had a job to do, and people were out there depending on us for protection and for being peacekeepers for the community. It did bring some satisfaction to me to bring some of these criminals to justice, and besides, I started to like this job.

I think it was at that time that I made the decision to branch out and do something different; something that would be a little more challenging and rewarding. At that time though, I had no idea what I wanted to do. Being an officer was a good job, with security and benefits. I know lots of guys who would have loved to have this job. I came to the realization that I had better stay where I was at that moment in time and in my life. This was mainly because I could not think of anything better that I wanted to do; and besides, I had grown to like this job.

By the time I settled down, and was progressing steadfastly forward in my work, I believed I had gained sufficient confidence in my abilities as a Police Officer and had resigned myself to do what it took to make my life a success as far as my job was concerned, but as far as my personal life was concerned, I was not where I wanted to be; however, two more years would pass by before an opportunity presented itself to me that would have life altering circumstances, as I made the move and migrated to the U.S.

OFFICER OF THE LAW

FAMILY LIFE

I was a single parent with a six-year-old daughter, and although I was employed and working, I was not financially stable. I lived at home with my mom, mainly because it was convenient for me to do so. It permitted me to see my daughter every day. I was away from home for about fourteen hours a day, five days a week, because of work. On many nights I would come home, and she would be asleep, but it was nice to see her sleeping, knowing she was safe. I was thankful that my mom was at home to take care of her while I was not there.

My weekends were spent with her. I took her everywhere I went, that way, mom could have the weekends off so she could take time off for herself. My daughter's mom had left the country for the U.S. much earlier, so I had to be dad and mom to our daughter.

Those were good times for us. I loved my daughter very much and did everything that I could to make her happy. We had fun together and I would look forward to spending my weekends with her. I believe that she did have a normal childhood, in spite of the fact that her mom was not around.

Her school was about eight miles away from home and walking was how she made it there. She was not alone. She was joined by other students who attended the same school, so the walk was not lonely for her as she made the trip back and forth each day. She did well in school and had good grades. It seemed as though she had a passion for learning, she always wanted to go to college.

Today, while living in the U.S. she had the opportunity to complete her higher education. It took several years to do so, but she finally made it. She never gave up the goal to go to college and complete her studies. I remember telling her when we were having one of our father daughter talks that when we do migrate to the U.S., she would have the opportunity to get it done. I was going to do everything in my power to make it happen for her. I did do this for her by being there for her and giving her all the support, she needed, so she would be able to complete her education.

FAMILY LIFE

MY HERO

My father was definitely my hero, but he was not a super person. He was just as ordinary as any other person that I knew. He was Caucasian, of Irish descent, and was born in Trinidad. He was tall, thin, had a very fair complexion, with black and grey wavy hair. He was a smoker, for he always had a cigarette in his mouth, and he could hold his liquor consumption; he could drink with anyone.

MY HERO

He was a hero to me because of his wisdom, his sincerity, his loyalty, and his forgiving nature. He used these qualities as events occurred during his lifetime to handle any situation that arose, he was a remarkable man.

ACCIDENTS

The stories about my dad comes to mind because they reinforce my belief that to me, he was truly a hero. He owned a car and this car was like he put it, his baby. He was always working on it, checking it out, cleaning it, and ensuring everything was in tip top shape, because that was his ride that took him, every day, back and forth to work.

On Boxing day, the day after Christmas Day, dad had me drive the car to the local store to pick up a few items for the house. Of course, he told me to be careful. I made my way to the shop and parked in front. Just as I was getting out of the car, another car came around the corner at a fast rate of speed and slammed into dad's car. The car got damaged badly but was still drivable.

I made my purchases and went home, fearing the wrath of my dad. I knew I was in trouble, because I was the one driving when it got hit, so in a way, it was my fault. Surprisingly, he was not that mad. He did rant and rave for quite a while, which made me feel very bad, but he made me promise that I would work with him to get it repaired.

The down part was after the car got repaired, I was not allowed to drive it anymore. I did not drive the car again for a whole year, but exactly one year to the date, I was once again allowed to go back to the same shop, on the same day, Boxing day, to once again purchase some items for the house.

I think because it was one year later, to the day, dad had forgotten that I had wrecked his car; however, I was very careful to drive in such a manner to insure nothing could happen to his car. I parked in front of the shop and went inside the store to make my purchases. While in the shop, I heard a car brakes squealing, followed by the sound of the impact as it slammed into something. I ran outside and was shocked and surprised to see that a car had crashed into dad's car causing damage.

I could not believe it, but there it was right before my eyes. I don't know what to call this one. How could this happen to me again? I could not explain it; how could this be? It was as though for whatever reason the first accident was not finished with me, and although I did not drive dads car for a whole year, whatever it was had been waiting for me to do the same thing I had done a year ago, just to show me that this can happen to me again. Fortunately, the car was still drivable, and I took it home. I explained it this way to myself, "It was somehow related to the fact that I was not supposed to ever drive dad's car," and as a matter of fact, I never drove his car again.

When I got home, and dad saw the car, I was surprised he took it so easy with me. He said that the second accident showed that I was not allowed to drive his car ever again, for it was a message from somewhere, but he never said where. Showing that this happened to prove his point that I should never drive his car. At that time, I believe he used one of his life values when he showed me forgiveness.

I promised to assist him in getting the car repaired, and together we brought it back to life as we called it. Back then we laughed about it, because how could, one year later, under the exact same circumstances, it gets hit again? Was that a coincidence or was it something else? I think it was an unexplained mystery, for there was no other way to explain it. I was very much surprised because dad was so forgiving of me, but that was the kind of dad he was.

FORESIGHT

I believed my father had foresight and good judgment, too. He wore glasses, stuttered when speaking, but could whistle a fine tune without missing a beat. After I graduated from High School, he said that I should become a mechanic just as him because I had the aptitude for it. I did not know it then, and did not see it, but he did.

Back then, I had tinkered with cars helping him working on them fixing and repairing small things, every now and then, usually just to help him. It was nice just to be in his company and to talk to him, usually about everything from family matters, politics, work, and little things that we run across in our daily life.

I remember these little talks with my dad as the good times in my life. Those times that we spent together in each other's company I have treasured, because life can be short, and we do not know the time or the hour that the Lord will call us to His table.

I did take dad's advice, as any good son should, and went to Trade School to become a mechanic. I am still in that profession today as an adult. I could not see it then, but somehow dad had. He had the wisdom to lead me in the right direction. This learned profession has served me well in my adult life, for today, this is how I have made my living and am able to provide and take care of myself and my family.

HONESTY

My dad was an honest person. I remember when I was about twelve years old, he came home from work with a wallet he found containing several hundred dollars and no identification. That was a lot of money in those days. When I found out about it, I said to him, "Dad, we should keep it and spend the money on ourselves, because it would be difficult to find the owner of the wallet," and dad said, "No, the money did not belong to us and we were not going to spend it." Over the next week or so, after work, he would make inquiries trying to find the owner of the wallet.

Eventually, he did find the owner and returned it to him after he made positive ID. Dad did not want anything for finding and returning the wallet. He said the man probably needed the money for himself and his family. The owner of the wallet was very grateful and offered to give dad some of the money for finding and returning his wallet to him, but dad did not take any money.

The gentleman said dad was the most honest person he had ever met. He also said that if someone else had found it, he did not think that person would have gone through all the trouble to find him and return his wallet; but that was the kind of person my dad was, and as we say, he was honest to the bone. Once again, he showed me another life value that he lived by.

LOYALTY

Dad spent a lot of time away from home working so that he could provide for our family. He said we were his number one priority in life. He never missed a day's work. No matter how bad the weather was or how sick he felt he was out there working, making that money. His faithfulness and devotion to our family is what really kept us together and kept us close. He will always be my hero.

He had the wisdom and foresight to see that I could be a mechanic. He showed us, by his example, what qualities it took to be an honest and honorable person by showing us how he dealt with the money he found. He proved his loyalty to the family by putting us first in his life and by going out there and providing for us.

I consider my dad to be a remarkable person. His qualities are his legacy to me. I have emulated them in my life and have

LOYALTY

passed them down to my children. So, through us, his memory will live on.

FORGIVENESS

Another thing that I remember about dad was his forgiving nature. I do not know how he did it, but I guess it was in his nature to do so. When I was younger, living on the cocoa and coffee plantation in Trinidad, he owned a truck which he used to transport material from the quarry to his clients.

One day, after the truck was loaded with material, dad parked the truck on the roadway in front of the office. The brake was on and the engine was running while he left it there and went inside to pick up some paperwork. While he was inside, his loader, the person who loads the truck, got behind the wheel of the truck and took off.

He attempted to drive up a hill, but the engine stopped and the truck rolled back and crashed into the nearby river bed, totally destroying the truck, and the truck bed; the cab was ripped off and the engine fell out. To me, this was a disaster and I believe the truck was done for and unfixable.

My dad, again being the top-notch mechanic that he was, was already thinking about repairing it. He did not get that mad. I believed he got a few shades redder and was very sad, broken hearted, and devastated, but although this would cost him a lot of money to repair, he forgave the loader and decided to repair the truck himself.

It took him months to fix the truck, but he did restore it back to how it was before the accident. He was indeed a very accomplished mechanic and I was amazed that he was able to do that and to forgive his loader, who could not drive, had no driver's license, no experience driving a truck, and he took it without dad's permission.

I saw dad as my hero because of his forgiving nature, mainly because of the things he has done for others without expecting anything in return, and the things that others has done to him, he has forgiven them all and held no animosity in his heart towards any one of them. It takes a very kindhearted and Godly person to do the things I saw him do, and I would say that he was a very special person.

He is gone now, having passed away in 1994. He was eighty-three years old, but I know he is missed by everyone who has come in contact with him over the years while he was alive. Long live the memory of my dad.

FORGIVENESS

DISCOVERY

I have combined all the information that I got over the years from my elder family members and I put them all together. Based on these facts, I came up with the best conclusion that I could, which would best answer my parent's heritage issue about moms' birth and early life, also about dad's heritage and his family life.

I found this necessary to do at this time, because all of my elder family members had passed away, except for my elder half-brother Freddie Julien, who, as I always say, is still alive and kicking.

All of the different stories that I have heard, from different family members over the years, have similarities in the sense that they all came from my grandfather, Charles Coombs. He was born in Barbados, an island in the Caribbean. Over the years, whenever he spoke to them, he would tell them only little bits and pieces about mom. Why his story about mom was slightly different every time he spoke to each one of them, I do not know.

I was younger then and myself and my grandfather were not that close, so he did not confide in me or any other family members. I believe his reluctance to talk to us about her was that maybe he did not want to tell us about her, maybe he believed that we could not handle that information about my mom. I remember him as being very quiet and reserved, you really had to pin him down if you wanted him to talk to you about anything, especially about mom.

Because the details of what he told each family member was slightly different, I found it necessary to speak to each one of them myself and write down what he told them, and what they told me he said. I could not understand what the issue was, but it must have been a sensitive subject for him to not want to speak openly about her, hence the little bits and pieces of information he gave to different family members. Was it because it was what he remembered at that time, or maybe he did not want it known that he had an affair and a baby with a Venezuelan Aborigine Indian woman during those years?

As I continued my research, I found out that my mom and her family came from the Orinoco, Delta Region of the Orinoco River in Venezuela. It was a swampy area and the people living there used boats for transportation along the river's tributaries. They lived in houses with thatched roofs and only a floor and no sides. These houses were built on stilts or tall posts, mainly because they were built on the banks of the river.

Her family were of the Buck Tribe, the name was a derivative of the Warao, or Warrau, or Guarauno, who were Nomadic South American Indians (Britannica.com). They were an indigenous group or tribe of people from Venezuela who, still today, inhabit some portions of the mangrove areas of the Orinoco Delta.

These people were short in stature and brown in complexion. My grandfather lived and worked close to that area, working on building roads. He employed one family, however you can only hire the whole family to take care of your needs. At the campsite they cooked and cleaned his area and also washed his clothes. Eventually, he got with my mom's mother, my grandmother. She became pregnant with my mom and my mom was born.

Sometime after the birth of my mom, the family, for whatever reason, left the baby on his bed in his camp and they left the area. One of the reasons they left may have been that she was not a full-blooded member of the tribe, so they moved on, probably to a different part of the delta. This is why after searching and inquiring about the family's whereabouts, he was unable to find them.

There was no one to care for the baby while he was at work, so he had to leave his job, take the baby and come to Trinidad. This is where she was raised. The rest of mom's childhood is sketchy, for I do not know much about her early childhood days and my grandfather did not want to talk about that part of her early childhood.

I don't see why mom's early life was such a secret. I have no information on that part of her life. I do not know if he got married or lived with someone, but there had to be a mother figure in her life to take care of her. I do not know who that was, and I do not know if grandpa ever got married, or if he had someone at his home to take care of her. I believe she was well taken care of, for she turned out to be the best mom to us and a very good wife to dad.

DISCOVERY

MIGRATION TO THE U.S.

It was early in the year 1976 when I decided to migrate to the US. I had a lot of thinking and soul searching to do before I could make such a decision. I did give this matter a lot of thought; there were many issues to work out, issues that could have an adverse effect on those whom I love if I decided to make that move. I knew moving would be hard for my daughter, she would be alone with my mom, her grandmother, and would not have her parent around.

When making a difficult decision, I found what worked best for me is to write down the pros and cons of the problem, go over it one item at a time, and eventually I will come up with a logical answer to the problem. I believe there was more to life and I had the faith necessary to make changes to my life. It was in times like this that one's faith is tested and I had to remember that I could not get anything accomplished without the help of the Lord, so I put my trust and faith in Him, knowing that He would guide my steps as I made plans to migrate to the U.S.

I did make the move to the United States. I put my mom in charge of my affairs and left my daughter with my mom and dad. The plan was for her to live with them until I could come back and get her. Financially I was not ready for the trip. I had enough money to purchase a two-way ticket to the U.S. and was left with only fifteen U.S. dollars in my pocket.

When I made the trip, I was stepping out on faith. It was the hardest thing I ever did. Here I was travelling to the U.S. with fifteen dollars in my pocket. I had an address where I was going but had no idea where it was or what to expect when I got there. I was totally dependent upon a friend to meet me at the airport and to take me to wherever I would be living. A thousand things were going through my mind as I got off the plane, "What if he did not show up to meet me, where would I go, and what would I do?"

Next, I remember the Immigration Officer asking me where I was going, how long was I staying in the country, and how was I going to make it with only fifteen dollars to my name. With so many questions, I had one of those moments of uncertainty, "Did I make the right decision in coming here? What if...?" there were a lot of *what if's*, but it was too late. Now I was committed. I was here and there was no turning back. I was in for the long haul and I was going to ride it out to the end.

I had knots in my stomach as an Immigration Officer escorted me back to *that* room. You know the one that leads through those double doors, the one that people disappear through? Well I was in that room for quite a while. I was asked a lot of questions. I think they were deciding whether or not they would let me into the country. The only thing I could tell them was that I had the name and address of the person that was picking me up, he would be responsible for my welfare, and I had a return ticket back to my home if things did not work out for me, as planned.

I did not know what would happen to me next, so I sat there and waited for the officer to return. Although what was going through my mind were negative thoughts like, "Would they let me into the country?" I believe the Lord was going to make a way for me to live and work here; so, I changed the way I was thinking, crossed my fingers, and trusted the Lord to make things right for me.

I was left alone in that room for a very long time, which seemed like an eternity. After a while, I heard my name announced through the overhead intercom system stating that my party was waiting for me in the reception area. I guess they believed me. Then right after that the officer returned and said I was free to go, all my fears went away, and I was relieved.

I felt the weight of uncertainty come off my shoulders. I stepped out of the airport, and although it was in the month of June it was cold, but I was ready to begin the next phase of my life. I thought about other foreigners, who years before, had come to this country seeking asylum and making the move to make a better life for themselves. The majority of them, like me, came here with nothing but the desire to work hard and make a better life for themselves and their families, and I was joining that group who paved the way for people like me.

I prayed and thanked the Lord for getting me this far. Where I was going, and what I was going to do with the rest of my life, was not yet written. I believed that was a good thing and I also believed that I could do whatever I wanted to. I was excited, I was in a new country with opportunities for anyone to make a better life for themselves, and I was ready to do what it took to make a spot in it, for me. I believe that my faith in the Lord increased at that time and I thank him, for without his help and guidance I would not have made it. All my praise and glory are to be given to the Lord Jesus Christ, for without His blessing, I would not have made it.

Sometimes, a person should step out on faith like I did, it worked for me, so I believe it would also work for them, if they are ever placed in that position in life. I was determined to get started with my plan to work hard, find a place to live, and do what it took to get my daughter into this country, so we could be together again. It took a while, but I was able to get her over here and have her live with me where she could also start a new chapter in her life.

FIRST U.S. JOB

After moving to California, a friend who I had recently met, told me of a job opportunity at an iron ore mine, where he worked. He took me there and I applied and got a job as a mechanic/welder, working through the local union. It was a good job. The pay and benefits were very good, so I settled down and worked very hard to prove to the company that I would be an asset to them.

I remember there were a lot of workers, like myself, employed there working in different crafts. We all lived in separate rooms in a single wide mobile home, placed side by side, which was converted into living quarters. A number of them were converted into bathrooms and showers. This type of living was new to me, but it was alright, and I easily adapted to that way of living.

FIRST U.S. JOB

The job itself was challenging. I did a lot of welding and auto mechanic repair work. It was what I had done before, so working there was very easy and fulfilling. I stayed employed and worked with this company until they went out of business. This job afforded me the opportunity to save enough money so I would become financially stable. After the company closed, I moved to Pahrump, a small town outside of Las Vegas, Nevada, and this was where my daughters attended school.

I started working my second job in the same field. I continued working for this new company and eventually retired from working there in December 2010. My employment here, in the U.S., has been great. I was able to stay on this job long enough to obtain a good retirement. For a person coming into the U.S. with $15.00 in cash, I was able to work hard and enjoy a good life, with family and close friends.

I proved to myself, and others too, that sometimes it is good to take that leap of faith. You would be amazed at what you can accomplish by doing so. Don't be afraid to explore new *Avenues of Adventures*, as I call it. The U.S. was founded by people just like me, all who were seeking a new life, in a strange land, for themselves and their families.

So, do like I did, be bold, be brave, and go forth and take your piece of the pie. I have learned that one can only get ahead if one is willing to go the extra mile and to travel the unbeaten path in life. Do not forget that it is not just your doing, for this can only happen if you put your trust and faith in the Lord. I realize that I alone did not accomplish what I have done in life, but everything I have done has come from the blessing of the Lord. I put my faith in Him, and He directed my steps and brought me to where I am today.

FIRST U.S. JOB

MILITARY TIME

To start a new life in a foreign country is not easy. A person, family, friend, or otherwise, will only do so much for you. Having to depend on another person to provide you with a place to stay, food to eat, and money to take care of other necessities is usually short lived, and was hard for me to accept, for in the past, I was always able to take care of myself.

I had always fended for myself and was not afraid to work. I knew how to do auto mechanic work, auto body repair, and painting. So, the first opportunity I got, I took a job doing just that. The work was hard. The hours were long, and it seems to me that it was always very cold. To me, Boston, Massachusetts, was always cold. Coming from the tropics to the U.S., the cold weather was a culture shock to me, so I can definitely say my first winter in the states was shocking, and of course, freezing.

MILITARY TIME

The money was good though, and with it I could purchase what I needed to make my life more comfortable and not impose on anyone. I made enough money to be able to send some home to mom, so she could take care of my daughter.

I also went to military training at Fort Dix in New Jersey. It was not what I expected it to be, but I was physically fit and able to endure the vigorous training and the cold weather, which prepared me for military life. After military training, being as I was attached to a reserve unit, I was transferred to California where I stayed for a few years. Eventually, I got a job in another part of the state and stayed there in my civilian job until that job shut down. I had to move to another state in pursuit of yet another job. This job was very lucrative, so I stayed there until my forced retirement in 2010.

During that time, I continued my military obligation duty, which was one weekend per month and two weeks in the summer. I was in the U.S. about six months when I first joined the U.S. Army and went off to my military training. I did not know what to expect with the change of weather that was coming, and me not having experienced or even seen snow before, but by the time I got out of military training, I was very comfortable in the snow and the coldness did not bother me as much, because I had learned how to tolerate it, how to dress for it, and how to survive in it.

I was physically fit. Because of the amount of physical activity and exercise I had to go through, the military training converted me and made me confident. It also gave me a purpose in life. I was a U.S. soldier and I was ready to fight for the country if the need arose.

I recall my first snowstorm. I was amazed, for it was the first time that I had seen snow. I remember getting dressed quickly and running outside to experience it. I was like a kid again, running through it, catching it as it fell from the sky, picking it up and running it through my fingers. It was fun for a while until I got cold. It was quite an experience.

Originally, I had joined the National Guard and after all of my training, I moved to California and then again to Nevada. I ended my military service at the rank of Master Sergeant, serving with the Army Reserve in Nevada during my career with the military, which spanned a period of thirty years. I completed two tours of duty in Germany and another three years of active duty state side at Fort Lewis in Washington, in support of Operation Enduring Freedom, Iraqi Freedom, and the War on Terrorism.

I obtained the necessary papers to bring my daughter, Desiree, into the U.S. I met and married her mom, here in the United States and had another daughter, Felicia, with her. So, when my elder daughter got here, she had a little sister waiting for her. It was a long time coming, but finally I had a home, a family, a wife, two kids, and a good civilian job too. I believed that finally I was where I wanted to be and was living the, much talked about, American dream.

This was one of the good times in my life. I settled down and worked hard to provide everything that was necessary to make a happy home for myself and my family. I can say that this was made possible because I joined the military, which also allowed me to bring my daughter into the U.S. It was long overdue, but finally, I was able to have her with me. All my praise and thanks go to the Lord, without whom this would not have happened.

Some of the benefits that one can receive from having served in the military is the education benefits. You can complete your education and also receive VA medical benefits, which covers the medical care and treatment of all military related injuries that you received during your service. So, being in the military can be rewarding, for you can learn a skill to use when your duty is over and you can take what you have learned in the military and use it to get into the civilian workforce.

Looking back, I could say that my move to the U.S. was a good one and stepping out on faith was also the wisest decision I had ever made.

DEATH OF MY FATHER

It was March 2003; I was still serving on active duty in the military. This activation duty was supposed to last one year, but as these things go, it lasted for three years. It was during that time when I got an assignment to go home to Trinidad on a military mission. At the conclusion of that mission, I stayed an additional ten days at home with my family. It was wonderful to see my mom and dad again and to spend time with them, for it has been a long time since I have seen them.

I stayed at home with them. I remember spending a lot of time with dad. He wanted to know how life was treating me while living abroad, so we talked about that, but mostly we just talked about everything, like his retirement, the family, his grandkids, and just about anything he wanted to.

I remember sitting with him in the downstairs portion of the house, in the garage, keeping him company while he worked on his car. It was a small car that he called his *baby*. Sometimes he would be fixing things under the hood of the car, underneath it, or sometimes inside it. I know this was what he liked to do, and he was most happy working on his little projects. I was happy to just be there with him. I would look at him as he worked on his car, as he smoked his cigarettes, and to me he looked happy and content, just doing that.

When I was younger, I always wondered why he spent so much time in and around his vehicle, just tinkering away. Now that I have become a mechanic and am older, I understood why dad loved it, because now I have been doing the same thing too, working on my auto projects. I guess in some ways I am just like my dad, for I am also happy when I work on my auto restoration projects.

Those ten days sure seemed to have gone by quickly, before I knew it, it was time to return back to the military. I was very thankful that I had the opportunity to go home and visit my mom and dad, for little did I know, that was the last time I would see him. One week later I received a phone call from home. My dad, Trevor Fahey, was dying, he passed away soon afterwards. Once again, I was on my way home, but this time it was no vacation. I was on my way to bury my dad.

I will forever treasure the memories of the last time I spent with him, our talks, our quiet times, and just being in each other's company. It is hard losing a parent, but years ago I made a decision to go abroad and seek my fortune. Dad was instrumental in helping me make that decision and I was incredibly grateful that he supported my decision and permitted me to leave.

Now that he was gone, I felt sad. On one hand, I knew he is in a better place, and in the other, I felt that I was not always there with him. Somehow, I knew I did the right thing and dad understood, for he was that kind of supportive parent.

DEATH OF MY FATHER

He is gone now; no longer with us, however my thoughts are always of him and I think of the legacy he has left behind for us to remember him by, and to live by. He always said the following,

"Life is made up of a series of decisions, and you should choose the one that you can live with, if you want to be remembered for the good decisions that you make."

Those words are in my heart and I try to live by them. I miss my dad, but he left a piece of himself with me that is in my heart and there it will remain as long as I shall live.

When I got the word that my dad was dying, at first, I was in denial, because one week earlier he was fine and healthy. He was hardly ever sick, and then suddenly, he was gone. The autopsy said he died of natural causes. I am grateful he passed without any pain or suffering, for he was a good father to us, loving, kind, and dedicated to his family and friends.

I know he lived a good life. He is missed by everyone who knew him, or in some way came in contact with him. I prayed the Lord would take him into His fold and give him peace.

With the passing of my dad I lost any kind of access that I could have gotten from him about his side of his family. I did not understand it, but he kept that side of his family closed off. He never spoke about his dad, his mom, or his uncles. So, I do not have any information about them, it is sad though, because I really wanted to know my roots, as far back as I can on his side of the family, but he is gone now and I would never know anything about that part of my family.

The only thing that is certain, is that he stood up for his family against all the prejudice that came his way, because of the fact that he was Caucasian, and mom was brown skinned. His family said she was black and was against him, but he married her anyway and stood his ground and stood up for his family. I should note that everyone who carries the name of

Fahey, in the country of Trinidad, can trace their roots back to mom and dad, for there is only one Fahey family name on the whole island, and now there are many of us with lots of grand and great grandchildren, carrying on the name of the Fahey family. I know he would have been proud to see how the family has grown and to know that it all started with him.

DEATH OF MY MOTHER

It was on the 12th of February 2013, I was still on active duty in the military when my mother, Hermina Fahey, passed and went to be with the Lord. I had to travel back to Trinidad to help make the necessary arrangements to bury her. She was 87 years old and was not a physically strong person. She was short in stature, brown in complexion, and was a small woman. She had a good life, but during her later years she was not always in good health, for she was plagued with a number of illnesses that kept her pretty much at home, except for her many doctor visits.

Oftentimes, she was well enough to get around. She had a good spirit, and for her age, she was strong but fragile, weighing only close to 100 lbs.; yet, she was well enough to have her daily strong black coffee, and of course would not shy away from a good strong alcoholic beverage. Also, during that time, she cooked her own meals.

As she neared her 87th birthday, her health deteriorated, and she spent more and more time in the hospital and visiting doctors. On February 12th, one day before her 87th birthday in 2013, she passed and went on to be with the Lord.

After dad passed, I know that my mom took his passing extremely hard. She would cry and talk fondly of him. They were inseparable, having been together for over seventy years. In every relationship there are misunderstandings, but no matter what the argument was about, at bedtime it was over, and they never went to sleep mad at each other. These are some of the small things I noticed and learned from my mom and have brought into my own marriage, and you know, it works. Every time I have the need to use it, I remember her, and it keeps her in my heart.

I knew there were moments when mom got lonely. We tried our best to encourage her to not give up on life, and to live for her children and grandchildren. I believe she did her best to be happy, but I knew she was still unhappy, for she missed dad a lot. I guess when you have been with someone for a lifetime and that person is no longer around, you would be very lonely too.

My mother, who unfortunately did not know her mother, had lived a good life. She had a loving husband, two daughters, five sons, lots of grand and great grandchildren. She was a joy to us all. I believe she did an excellent job raising me and my siblings, for I believe we all turned out ok.

I remember her as a strict disciplinarian who put family first in her life. She had many friends, young and old, and was very well respected in the village by all. She would be missed by everyone who had the pleasure of knowing her. It would have been nice for her to have known something about her mom before her passing, but as it stood back then, she never did find out anything about her. I believe her legacy to us is what she told us many times over the years, and that was for us not to judge anyone unless you have given them the chance to prove themselves first.

I also remember the things that she told me when I started dating girls, which was, "Don't buy cat in bag." At the time I did not give it much thought, but every time I told her about another girl that I had met, she would tell me the same thing, "Don't buy cat in bag."

I finally asked her what that statement meant, and she said it meant that I should not start a relationship or get involved with a girl and not know anything about her and her family. I now believe that was good advice to follow, but of course, I did not do so. Looking back, with all the broken relationship I have had in my life, I should have taken her advice.

Another saying my mother had, and told me many times was, "When you are in good house, bad house comes calling." She said it meant, your bad friends will call you out of your good house and get you in trouble. Of course, I did not heed her warning and found myself in trouble.

I will treasure the things she always said to me, for it is a good way to remember her. May the good Lord bless her and keep her in that better place.

DEATH OF MY MOTHER

THE WAKE

In Trinidad, Mom's funeral, as well as dads, followed the local traditional way. The home of the deceased family provided alcohol and food to everyone who came to the house for the "Wake." This is a brief explanation of what folks usually do when they come to the house for the wake. They would stay up all night and day, this goes on from the announcement of the death of the person, until the day of the funeral.

Usually tents are set up in the front of the house for people to sit under just in case it rained. Tables are also set up under the tents for people to play card games. The most favorite game is called *All Fours*. Another thing that is done is called *Beating Bamboo*. This is when bamboo is cut, about four to five feet long, the fatter the bamboo the better the sound, I was told. This beating of the bamboo is done only at night and usually by a number of people, young or old, male or female, or a mixture of both. They would gather somewhere in the yard of the house, get in a circle, and would sing traditional songs while beating on the bamboo with sticks and hitting it on the ground. Doing this kept the rhythm going. It is amazing, but they come up with some songs that are very melodious.

Within the circle of the bamboo beaters and singers, a bottle of rum is placed on the ground with several cups so the singers and bamboo beaters can stop and have an occasional drink. Another thing that is placed within the circle of folks is a bottle with kerosene and a cloth wick inside it, which is lit to provide light, this is called a "flambeau."

The beating of the bamboo can go on nightly until the day of the burial. This, I believe, is considered a part of the celebration of the deceased person's life as they make their journey to a better life with the Lord.

THE BIG "C"

In 2007, I finally retired from military service, having completed my military obligation. At that time, I was also diagnosed with the beginning stages of Multiple Myeloma, which is cancer of the bone marrow in the body. No treatment was necessary at that time; however, I had to be monitored every six months to see if it was progressing, but as the cancer progressed, monitoring changed to every three months, then monthly.

I continued working my civilian job for another three years. By then my cancer had reached the stage where my Oncologist suggested that because of the progression of my cancer, I had to retire from working. So, I was forced to retire at the end of 2010. I had faith in the Lord and faith in healing, for faith heals and faith cures all. I began weekly visits with an Oncologist at UCLA in Los Angeles, California.

For two days as I had to begin actual chemo treatments, my cancer was progressing steadily, so my Oncologist decided that my cancer had progressed to the stage where a Stem Cell Transplant had to be done. Stem cells were harvested from my blood. The damaged cells were removed, and the good cells were frozen, and during the Stem Cell Transplant procedure the good stem cells were put back into my body. Using my own stem cells was the only proven way to do the Stem Cell Transplant for what I needed.

This procedure was then performed in April 2018. during that time, I stayed at an apartment close to UCLA for two months, because I had to be in the hospital every day for 10 to 12 hours. I was the first cancer patient to have this transplant procedure done on an outpatient basis at UCLA. The chemo I received was terrible. It lowered my resistance to zero, so when they reintroduced my clean blood cells back into my body, I had to be monitored daily to make sure my body was accepting the new cells, and that my red blood cells were growing back.

During my daily stay at the hospital, while being treated, I could get some sleep in my bed, but during the night, while back at the apartment, I had a horrible time and was unable to sleep. I was also unable to eat or hold anything down, even drinking water caused me to vomit and gave me diarrhea, although I did not have too much food in my stomach. The chemo caused ulcers in my mouth and throat, so my mouth was a horrible mess. I even had to have help sitting and getting up off the toilet. I was very weak and had to have my wife, Brenda, help me do everything. I am blessed to have a wife like her, she had to give me my daily shower, dry me off, and dress me. God bless her, for she stayed with me 24 hours a day.

Thank God for my wife and family, for without them I could not have taken the stem cell transplant and come through it. The sacrifice, support, and prayers I received from my wife, Brenda, my kids, Desiree, Tyanna, Breanna, and Felicia, my pastor, Jarvis Hines, who took time off from his ministry to come and be with me, my friend, Randy Taylor, who also took time off from his job to come and be with me, were all God driven and I am very grateful to all of them.

To my other friends who were unable to come to UCLA, but sent their love and prayers, I thank you all. It is nice to know that I have so many friends and well-wishers who care for me, God bless you all.

I was finally released from the hospital and allowed to go home, but with many restrictions like staying away from crowds and sick people, and having a clean and sanitized place to stay in. At that time, my cancer had gone into remission, but I still had to do weekly visits to the hospital, for what the Oncologist said was *maintenance chemo treatments*. This changed to every 2 weeks but continued for 1 year.

At the end, my cancer was still in remission. All of my blood levels and blood counts were normal, so I believe that with the grace of God, the prayers, and the belief that the Lord will heal me, I am healed from the Multiple Myeloma Cancer and I am able to live a normal life.

All praise, honor, and glory go to my Lord, Jesus Christ, who I believe healed me of my Multiple Myeloma Cancer. I know that the Lord was the one who healed me. I have to give special thanks to my wife, Brenda, who was there with me, taking care of me 24 hours a day and Apostle Jarvis Hines who was also there with me praying and ministering to me, ensuring that as I go through this procedure I kept my faith in the Lord. Well, I did keep the faith and the end result was the Lord healed me of the cancer.

At my church, together with my wife, I gave my testimony about what the Lord has done for me and how he healed me. I hope that by letting them know what the Lord did for me, they would believe in the Lord like I did, because if He can heal me of my cancer, all you have to do is put your faith in the Lord and whatever you pray for He will give to you, for that is the kind of Lord we have. So, show him your love and obedience and He will take care of you, too.

EFFECTS OF 9 / 11

In March 2011, I was in college working on my bachelor's degree. The English professor wanted to know how 9/11 affected us, as military personnel; He wanted the twelve of us in the class to write a paper on how we were affected by 9/11 and made this a part of our curriculum. We all completed this assignment and after we turned our papers in, we decided to get together to discuss how each of us dealt with the effects of 9/11 and how it affected us.

The things that happened to us when we returned home was very sad, but on the other hand, it was very enlightening because the effects of 9/11 affected us all in different ways. It was interesting to hear the different eye opening and heart wrenching stories, but each of us all had a few things in common; we returned home after active duty to find broken families, broken marriages, and badly in debt.

I had to give everyone credit for the fact that they recognized where they stood at that time, and what they were going to do to get back to their life, as it was before 9/11. It was amazing to see that they never gave up on life; I wondered if it was because of the military training we all received, which helped us, or was it something else, because we all picked ourselves up and moved on.

It was amazing to hear those stories. One of us was not there for the birth of his child, another came home to find his spouse living in his home with another person, another came home to find his spouse gone, she had moved to another state; so, he came home to an empty house. Another came home to find himself on the brink of disaster. While we are on active duty we are protected from repossession, but the minute we are off, everything becomes due and payable; so, having no cash on hand he found himself on the streets due to bad money management, for he had sent all of his income home to his spouse, but she did not take care of business. There was no money when he got back home.

All the stories we shared that day were very similar. In my case when I came home, and like the other soldiers, I found myself badly in debt too. I had no money in the bank and had a broken marriage. Although we all sent money home to our spouses, faithfully, twice a month, only a couple of us came home and found that while they were away, their spouses had stood up and taken care of the family and their finances.

You can see that we all had similar stories as we talk to each other about our issues. Before we parted we discovered that we all had one thing in common and spoke about it openly and it was nice to have taken the time to sit down and minister to each other, as vets, who were all going through the same thing. It afforded us the opportunity to vent and to talk about our problems with one another, who all went through similar issues, and to release some of the pent-up emotions to other soldiers who could understand our issues.

I believe that our meeting went very well, we left there feeling much better with ourselves and had decided to occasionally check with each other to see how things were going. Something else that came out of the meeting was that we were ready to start our lives over again, and no matter what position in life we were in at that time, if we were ever called up to go back into active duty, or to any other situation that required our military expertise, we would not hesitate to jump right back in and fight for our country.

In my case, I was activated and deployed to Fort Lewis, Washington, during the Operation Enduring Freedom (OEF) conflict. At the time, my home was in Las Vegas, Nevada. My initial tour of duty was for one year. I was attached to an Army Reserve Unit that was a Reserve Medical Unit and was given a week to get our affairs in order before we left.

I had a good paying job, so my spouse and I sat down and decided how we were going to handle the loss of income while

I was away. So, by the time I left, we had come up with a plan of action. We figured that with the money I would send home, and the other income that she got from her job, she would have enough money to take care of the finances and our home, and still have enough money left over so she could put some away for a rainy day.

My deployment was extended twice, so I was away for over three years, but things did not turn out as planned, and as a result, when I returned home, I found myself in a financial dilemma. The impact of the financial situation that personally affected me after my deployment was the damage to my credit. Even though I made arrangements to make payments to correct my pass due accounts, the damage was done, and the adverse negative credit report entries would stay with me, in some cases as long as seven years.

I returned home to a family that had ill feelings towards each other and it took a long time to mend things between us. I knew it was hard on my family while I was deployed, but I was hoping and praying that everything will be fine when I got back home.

So, what was the impact that 9/11 had on my life? Well, for one, I will forever live with the knowledge that I did satisfy my military obligation. I am a soldier; the country was at war and I had to do what was necessary. I returned home, after my deployment, to a broken home, animosity between family members, lack of trust between my spouse and I, badly in debt, no cash on hand, and a broken marriage. Those things were the most important things to me then; so, 9/11 did have a negative impact on my life.

My deployment had changed my life for a number of years. I took it hard at that time, but with counseling, I was able to forgive and put everything back in perspective, behind me, and move ahead with my life. I was ready to start the rebuilding process. There was much to do, and I was quite ready to start.

Eventually I was able to get my finances back on track, but my marriage was over. Although these things caused problems in my life, I was able to pick myself up and start over. I finally got to a point in my life where I was able to feel like a little normalcy had come back to me, which made me feel that everything was going to be alright.

EFFECTS OF 9/11

CATHOLICISM

It is my belief that the Catholic Church believes that the bible is the inspired, error free, and the revealed Word of God (Catholicism For Dummies, 3rd Edition). I totally agree with that and found that sometimes as we go through life, we settle for where we are, not knowing how to move ahead. The Lord does not want us to stay in one place. When you realize you are down in the pits and think that things would never get better for you, this is the time the Lord will open a way for you. All you have to do is to trust Him, believe in Him, and step out on faith.

I grew up in the Catholic Church, mainly because this was the church that myself and my family attended back at home on the island. While I was growing up in the church, my mom and dad made sure that my brothers, and sisters, and I did what was required of us to remain in the faith, by us taking the necessary religious instruction to get our first communion and confirmation. After that, we were required to attend church as much as possible as I grew up. Somehow, I got away from the faith. I did not find time to attend church or follow the faith, but I believe, that in me the faith in the Lord was still there in my heart.

Later on, in order to make the move to the U.S., I prayed to the Lord and put my trust in Him, asking for His help, and His guidance as I prepared to make my decision to go abroad. I did make my decision to move and I put my trust in Him and stepped out on faith. After moving to the U.S. I joined the military, but still was not a regular church goer and did not have a close relationship with anyone in the church.

After getting out of active duty and going back into the reserves, I spent about six years in a small town in California working at an iron ore mine, but there was no church there; so, during those years I did not attend any church. I did my best to live an honorable life by doing what was right, but deep inside of me, I always thought that something was missing where the Lord was concerned.

I moved again, working in another small town in Nevada and joined a Catholic Church. I was determined to get back into the church and get closer to the Lord. Everything went well, but my faith was really tested when my marriage broke up. I have to mention that when I got married, I did not do so in the Catholic Church, for being in the church, one is required to get married in the church and I did not do so. Those were trying times, but with prayer I made it through the rough times.

Several years later, I moved to Las Vegas, Nevada, and joined another church there and stayed in the church. Being in the church helped me to deal with the frustration that comes with a broken family life, but there were a number of religious programs available to help members who needed spiritual guidance, and these programs and classes were a life saver for me. They got me back on the right track and I was able to get back into the church and to be closer with the Lord.

Now, I don't have anything negative to say about the Catholic Church, because I grew up in this faith and it was what I believed in. They were there for me when I needed spiritual guidance, and at the time, it was a life saver. The Catholic Church has been good to me.

CHRISTIAN FAITH

Sometime later, I eventually married again. This time it was to a Christian woman, Brenda, who followed a Christian Church. I had the opportunity to attend a service with her, at her church, and I was introduced to the pastor. I was really touched at the way the service was conducted, the way the sermon was explained, and to see and feel the Spirit of the Lord in the church. I then decided to become a member of this church.

I liked the way the sermons were bible based and the pastor, Apostle Jarvis Hines, took time to counsel and teach each, and every, member in the church about the Lord. It was very uplifting, and I wanted to become a part of this ministry. Needless to say, I stayed in this Christian church and no longer attended the Catholic Church. Being a part of this Christian Church made me feel closer to the Lord. I got to really know the word and felt much closer to Him.

Everything returned back to normal and I settled down in my new church life, my home life, and my marriage. My wife and I continue to be active members of the church, and it is very fulfilling to us to be a part of this ministry.

DEATH OF MY GRANDSON

I was content with my life during this time, but I did not know that my peace was about to be broken, and my faith would be tested. I had a close relationship with my one and only grandson, Raheem. At that time, he was in his last year of college, and would be graduating in the field of Kinesiology.

One Saturday night in June 2018, around 10:30 PM, I was talking to my eldest daughter, Desiree, just keeping in touch with the family. I remember talking to Raheem and he said he was getting dressed, because his friend invited him to go to a house party. We had our phone on speaker and I heard him ask his mom how he looked, referring to how he was dressed for the party. He told me he had to finish getting dressed, so I told him to have fun and that I would talk to him tomorrow.

Little did I know that I was speaking to him for the last time, and within 2 hours of our conversation, he would be murdered in a drive by shooting at the place where the party was being held. I felt like I was in a dream. How could this happen? Having just spoken to my grandson and to know that the Lord had taken him away. I asked the Lord why, but you know He works in mysterious ways, and we do not know the ways of the Lord; we are only to trust Him, for He knows best.

This was a shock to the family, and we all took this extremely hard, but we all got together and did what we had to do to give him the best homecoming ever. I believed then, that he went up to a better place to rest and to be with the Lord. It was good to see that the whole family came out and supported his homecoming and were also there providing emotional support to his immediate family. Many of his friends also came and supported the family. It was amazing to see them all there. It was evident that he had many friends, and that he was loved and respected by them.

DEATH OF MY GRANDSON

MEMORIES

The fondest memories of my grandson, Raheem, that I remember was during the summer before his death. His mom got him a car that needed an engine. He wanted to work on it, so together we bought a rebuilt engine. We took the old engine out, switched out the parts we needed from the old engine to the rebuilt engine, and installed the engine back into the car.

I am a mechanic by trade, and my grandson wanted to do everything in his car himself, because he was interested in learning auto mechanics. He had the mechanical aptitude, so I allowed him to do just about everything on his own. He asked many questions and I helped him with the technical parts, which I let him do with my guidance. I was there to encourage and guide him and he did very well. He was okay with getting his hands dirty and learning how things work on an engine and how the different parts all work together. When we were done and we were ready to start the engine for the first time, he got very excited and I remember the look of amazement and satisfaction on his face as he listened to the purring of the engine. Just looking at him brought great pleasure to me. This memory of him will forever stay in my heart.

It was exciting for him too, because he did all the work of putting his car together. I could see how proud he was knowing that he did it with only technical assistance from me, and like I told him, "I am very proud of you for how hard you worked on your car."

That being said, the repairs were done, and we were ready to test drive the car on the freeway. I let him drive first. He drove the car very carefully, but as his confidence picked up, he soon brought the car up to speed. He was amazed at how the car performed, and after thanking me for my assistance in completing this project, he was ready to return home.

He had taken the summer off, just to come and work on his

car so it would be ready for school. He was pleased and happy and so was I. Together, we completed quite a project, and looking back, I was really excited to have him spend the summer with me while we worked on his project. You know, it was pleasing to me to have spent time with him, my one and only grandson.

In our everyday lives, we tend to get so busy with our daily life issues that we tend to put family affairs on the back burner, so it was good to have us come together and spend time with each other. These memories will always remain in my heart, for this was the last summer we spent together.

MEMORIES

BAPTISM

Sometime later, I did some soul searching. I believed that life was short, but what really touched me was the fact that I did not know where my grandson stood with his faith in the Lord, and whether or not he was saved. I spoke with my Pastor, Apostle Jarvis Hines, and he ministered to us, the whole family, about getting everyone baptized. He reasoned that this was the best way to get us to know the Lord and to follow His teaching.

The baptism is only the first step on having a relationship with the Lord, for after baptism, we are to continue reading the word, attending church, and living the life that Christ would want us to live. So, my family and I all got baptized. This included me, my spouse, three of my daughters, my three grandchildren, my brother-in-law, his spouse, their children, and grandchildren, and a few of my close friends. All seventeen of us were baptized that day. It was a glorious and blessed day to see my family getting baptized and to know that because of my grandson's death and wanting to know if he was saved, my family was now baptized, and they were on their way to being one with the Lord.

I never looked into the faith of my family before then. It took a tragedy, like the death of my grandson, to bring to light the fact that as the head of the family I am also responsible for the welfare and salvation of my family. Yes, my grandson's death was terrible, hurtful, and a tragedy to the family, but out of this unfortunate incident, and my desire to know where my family stood with the Lord, I was able to bring them all closer to the Lord through baptism.

I must thank my Apostle, Jarvis Hines, for being there with my family and guiding us as we went through this. I give all thanks, praise, and glory to the Lord, for without him I would not have been able to do this. I continue to influence my family by having them read their bibles, going to church, living the Christian life, and developing a closer relationship with the Lord.

My wife, Brenda, and I continue to be active members of the church. With the guidance of our Apostle we are studying the word and supporting the ministry. We are doing everything we can to further advance the mission of the church, which is to go out and reach as many people as possible, to get them back into church, teach them the word, and make them believers in the Lord and His word.

BAPTISM

BIBLIOGRAPHY

The Warao People – www.britannica.com

The Orinoco river South America – www.britannia.com

The Orinoco River Delta – www.orinoco-delta.net

Where Is Trinidad and Tobago – www.worldatlas.com

www.ingramcontent.com/pod-product-compliance
Lightning Source LLC
Chambersburg PA
CBHW051836090426
42736CB00011B/1836